סִדּוּר קָטָן
Siddur Katan

Shabbat Prayer Book
For Families With Young Children
A Component of the Minyan Katan Shabbat Service

by
Jaime Lewis
with Michelle V. Katz

Editorial Committee:
Hannah Tobin Cohen
Rabbi David E. Levy

ISBN: 978-0-87441-909-2
©2013 by KidsCan Music LLC
Design and Art: Project Design LLC
Project Editor: Terry S. Kaye
Manufactured in the United States of America

Behrman House, Inc.
www.behrmanhouse.com

Contents

WELCOME

Shabbat Shalom　　שַׁבָּת שָׁלוֹם

Have a blessed and peaceful Shabbat.

Shabbat shalom, Shabbat shalom,　　שַׁבָּת שָׁלוֹם, שַׁבָּת שָׁלוֹם
Shabbat shalom u'm'vorach　x2　　2x　שַׁבָּת שָׁלוֹם וּמְבוֹרָךְ

Yai dai dai dai, yai dai dai dai, yai dai dai dai dai

Yai dai dai dai, yai dai dai dai

Shabbat shalom u'm'vorach　　שַׁבָּת שָׁלוֹם וּמְבוֹרָךְ

It's Shabbat

It's Shabbat—I can feel it in my head/*rosh*　x3
Shabbat shalom hay!

It's Shabbat—I can feel it in my hands/*yadayim*　x3
Shabbat shalom hay!

Legs/*raglayim*; belly/*beten*; heart/*leiv*
It's Shabbat—I can feel it with my friends/*chaveirim*　x3
Shabbat shalom hay!

It's Time to Make the Challah

It's time to make the challah
We'll mix and mix and mix
We'll knead and knead and let it rise
Then braid it in a twist

First we'll add the water
We'll mix and mix and mix….

Additional verses: flour, oil, eggs, sugar/honey

Ending: We'll put it in the oven to bake and bake and bake
And then at Shabbat dinner, the Motzi we will make

You'll Never Guess

You'll never guess who I met near synagogue/shul/temple today.
Well, I met a duck, he had some friends, and here's what they had to say:
Quack, quack, quack, Shabbat shalom, Shabbat shalom to you.   x2

Quack!

You'll never guess who I met near synagogue/shul/temple today.
Well, I met a cow, she had some friends, and here's what they had to say:
Moo, moo, moo, Shabbat shalom, Shabbat shalom to you.   x2

Moo!

Additional verses: monkey—oo oo ah ah, lion—roar, sheep—baa

MORNING PRAYERS

Modeh/Modah Ani	מוֹדֶה/מוֹדָה אֲנִי

Thank You, God, for bringing my soul back to me.

Modeh/Modah ani l'fanecha

מוֹדֶה/מוֹדָה אֲנִי לְפָנֶיךָ

Melech chai v'kayam

מֶלֶךְ חַי וְקַיָּם

Shehechezarta bi nishmati b'chemlah

שֶׁהֶחֱזַרְתָּ בִּי נִשְׁמָתִי בְּחֶמְלָה

Rabah emunatecha

רַבָּה אֱמוּנָתֶךָ

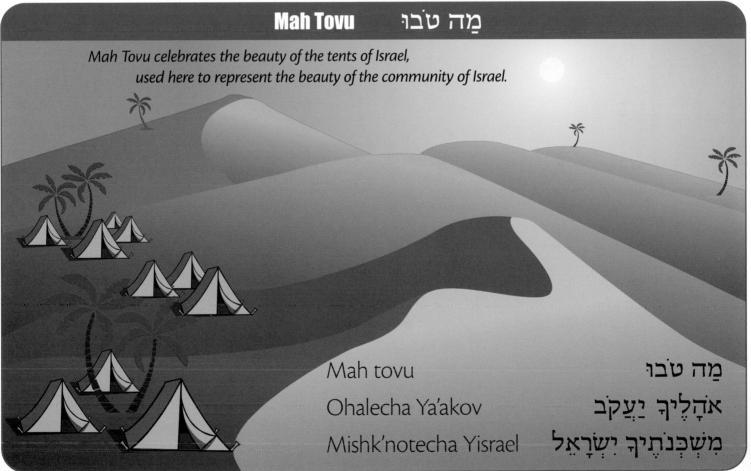

Mah Tovu מַה טֹּבוּ

*Mah Tovu celebrates the beauty of the tents of Israel,
used here to represent the beauty of the community of Israel.*

Mah tovu — מַה טֹּבוּ

Ohalecha Ya'akov — אֹהָלֶיךָ יַעֲקֹב

Mishk'notecha Yisrael — מִשְׁכְּנֹתֶיךָ יִשְׂרָאֵל

In Hal'lu, we praise God in different ways.
We sing of praising God with musical instruments, such as flutes and cymbals.
We marvel that the breath of every creature praises God.

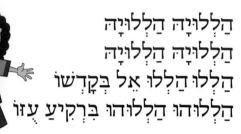

Hal'luyah, hal'luyah
Hal'luyah, hal'luyah
Hal'lu, hal'lu Eil b'kodsho
Hal'luhu, hal'luhu birki'a uzo

הַלְלוּיָה הַלְלוּיָה
הַלְלוּיָה הַלְלוּיָה
הַלְלוּ הַלְלוּ אֵל בְּקָדְשׁוֹ
הַלְלוּהוּ הַלְלוּהוּ בִּרְקִיעַ עֻזּוֹ

Hal'luhu, hal'luhu
Hal'luhu, hal'luhu
Hal'luhu, hal'luhu bigvurotav
Hal'luhu, hal'luhu k'rov gudlo

הַלְלוּהוּ הַלְלוּהוּ
הַלְלוּהוּ הַלְלוּהוּ
הַלְלוּהוּ הַלְלוּהוּ בִּגְבוּרֹתָיו
הַלְלוּהוּ הַלְלוּהוּ כְּרֹב גֻּדְלוֹ

Hal'luhu, hal'luhu
Hal'luhu, hal'luhu
Hal'luhu, hal'luhu b'teika shofar
Hal'luhu, hal'luhu b'neivel v'chinor

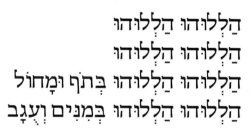

הַלְלוּהוּ הַלְלוּהוּ
הַלְלוּהוּ הַלְלוּהוּ
הַלְלוּהוּ הַלְלוּהוּ בְּתֵקַע שׁוֹפָר
הַלְלוּהוּ הַלְלוּהוּ בְּנֵבֶל וְכִנּוֹר

Hal'luhu, hal'luhu
Hal'luhu, hal'luhu
Hal'luhu, hal'luhu b'tof umachol
Hal'luhu, hal'luhu b'minim v'ugav

הַלְלוּהוּ הַלְלוּהוּ
הַלְלוּהוּ הַלְלוּהוּ
הַלְלוּהוּ הַלְלוּהוּ בְּתֹף וּמָחוֹל
הַלְלוּהוּ הַלְלוּהוּ בְּמִנִּים וְעֻגָב

Hal'luhu, hal'luhu
Hal'luhu, hal'luhu
Hal'luhu, hal'luhu b'tziltz'lei shama
Hal'luhu, hal'luhu b'tziltz'lei t'ru'ah

הַלְלוּהוּ הַלְלוּהוּ
הַלְלוּהוּ הַלְלוּהוּ
הַלְלוּהוּ הַלְלוּהוּ בְּצִלְצְלֵי שָׁמַע
הַלְלוּהוּ הַלְלוּהוּ בְּצִלְצְלֵי תְרוּעָה

Kol ha'n'shamah t'haleil Yah, hal'luyah
Kol ha'n'shamah t'haleil Yah, hal'luyah

כֹּל הַנְּשָׁמָה תְּהַלֵּל יָהּ הַלְלוּיָה
כֹּל הַנְּשָׁמָה תְּהַלֵּל יָהּ הַלְלוּיָה

Please rise and face the Ark.

Bar'chu בָּרְכוּ

In Bar'chu, we praise God as the source of all blessings for all time.
We praise God, Creator of light and darkness, Maker of peace, and Creator of all things.

Leader:

Bar'chu et Adonai ha'm'vorach

בָּרְכוּ אֶת יְיָ הַמְבֹרָךְ

Congregation:

Baruch Adonai ha'm'vorach l'olam va'ed

בָּרוּךְ יְיָ הַמְבֹרָךְ לְעוֹלָם וָעֶד

Leader:

Baruch Adonai ha'm'vorach l'olam va'ed

בָּרוּךְ יְיָ הַמְבֹרָךְ לְעוֹלָם וָעֶד

Leader & Congregation:

Baruch Atah Adonai Eloheinu Melech ha'olam

בָּרוּךְ אַתָּה יְיָ אֱלֹהֵינוּ מֶלֶךְ הָעוֹלָם

Yotzeir or uvorei choshech

יוֹצֵר אוֹר וּבוֹרֵא חֹשֶׁךְ

Oseh shalom uvorei et hakol

עֹשֶׂה שָׁלוֹם וּבוֹרֵא אֶת הַכֹּל

Let a new light shine on Zion,
and may we all be
able to see its beauty.
Praised are You, God, who makes the light.

Or chadash al Tziyon ta'ir   x2   2x   אוֹר חָדָשׁ עַל צִיּוֹן תָּאִיר

V'nizkeh chulanu m'heirah l'oro   x2   2x   וְנִזְכֶּה כֻלָּנוּ מְהֵרָה לְאוֹרוֹ

Baruch Atah Adonai   בָּרוּךְ אַתָּה יְיָ

Yotzeir ham'orot   יוֹצֵר הַמְּאוֹרוֹת

Sh'ma   שְׁמַע

The people of Israel are told to hear as the Sh'ma proclaims God's oneness and God's greatness forever.

Sh'ma Yisrael Adonai Eloheinu Adonai echad

שְׁמַע יִשְׂרָאֵל יְיָ אֱלֹהֵינוּ יְיָ אֶחָד

Baruch sheim k'vod malchuto l'olam va'ed

בָּרוּךְ שֵׁם כְּבוֹד מַלְכוּתוֹ לְעוֹלָם וָעֶד

In the V'ahavta, we are instructed to love God with all of our heart, might, and soul.
We are told to teach these words to our children, to think of them wherever we are, before we go to sleep
and when we wake up. We are to wear reminders of these words on our hands and head (in tefillin).
We are to write them on our doorposts and gates (in mezuzot).

V'ahavta et Adonai Elohecha

וְאָהַבְתָּ אֵת יְיָ אֱלֹהֶיךָ

b'chol l'vav'cha uv'chol nafsh'cha uv'chol m'odecha

בְּכָל לְבָבְךָ וּבְכָל נַפְשְׁךָ וּבְכָל מְאֹדֶךָ

V'hayu had'varim ha'eileh

וְהָיוּ הַדְּבָרִים הָאֵלֶּה

asher anochi m'tzavcha hayom al l'vavecha

אֲשֶׁר אָנֹכִי מְצַוְּךָ הַיּוֹם עַל לְבָבֶךָ

V'shinantam l'vanecha v'dibarta bam

וְשִׁנַּנְתָּם לְבָנֶיךָ וְדִבַּרְתָּ בָּם

B'shivt'cha b'veitecha uv'lecht'cha vaderech

בְּשִׁבְתְּךָ בְּבֵיתֶךָ וּבְלֶכְתְּךָ בַדֶּרֶךְ

Uv'shochb'cha uv'kumecha

וּבְשָׁכְבְּךָ וּבְקוּמֶךָ

Uk'shartam l'ot al yadecha

וּקְשַׁרְתָּם לְאוֹת עַל יָדֶךָ

V'hayu l'totafot bein einecha

וְהָיוּ לְטֹטָפֹת בֵּין עֵינֶיךָ

Uch'tavtam al m'zuzot beitecha uvish'arecha

וּכְתַבְתָּם עַל מְזֻזוֹת בֵּיתֶךָ וּבִשְׁעָרֶיךָ

Who can compare in power or holiness to God, who does awesome deeds?

Mi chamochah ba'eilim Adonai

Mi kamochah nedar bakodesh

Nora t'hilot oseh fele

מִי כָמֹכָה בָּאֵלִם יְיָ

מִי כָמֹכָה נֶאְדָּר בַּקֹּדֶשׁ

נוֹרָא תְהִלֹּת עֹשֵׂה פֶלֶא

Amidah עֲמִידָה

*We praise God—our God, and God of our forefathers Abraham, Isaac,
and Jacob [and our foremothers Sarah, Rebecca, Rachel, and Leah].
God is great and strong. God remembers all that our ancestors
have done and will bring a redeemer to their children.
Praised are You, God, the shield of Abraham and guardian/helper of Sarah.*

Baruch Atah Adonai
בָּרוּךְ אַתָּה יְיָ

Eloheinu v'eilohei avoteinu [v'imoteinu]
אֱלֹהֵינוּ וֵאלֹהֵי אֲבוֹתֵינוּ [וְאִמּוֹתֵינוּ]

Elohei Avraham Elohei Yitzchak v'eilohei Ya'akov
אֱלֹהֵי אַבְרָהָם אֱלֹהֵי יִצְחָק וֵאלֹהֵי יַעֲקֹב

[Elohei Sarah Elohei Rivkah Elohei Rachel v'eilohei Le'ah]
[אֱלֹהֵי שָׂרָה אֱלֹהֵי רִבְקָה אֱלֹהֵי רָחֵל וֵאלֹהֵי לֵאָה]

Ha'Eil hagadol hagibor v'hanora Eil elyon
הָאֵל הַגָּדוֹל הַגִּבּוֹר וְהַנּוֹרָא אֵל עֶלְיוֹן

Gomeil chasadim tovim v'koneih hakol
גּוֹמֵל חֲסָדִים טוֹבִים וְקוֹנֵה הַכֹּל

V'zocheir chasdei avot [v'imahot]
וְזוֹכֵר חַסְדֵי אָבוֹת [וְאִמָּהוֹת]

Umeivi go'eil [ge'ulah] livnei v'neihem
וּמֵבִיא גוֹאֵל [גְּאֻלָּה] לִבְנֵי בְנֵיהֶם

L'ma'an sh'mo b'ahavah
לְמַעַן שְׁמוֹ בְּאַהֲבָה

Melech ozeir [ufokeid] umoshi'a umagein
מֶלֶךְ עוֹזֵר [וּפוֹקֵד] וּמוֹשִׁיעַ וּמָגֵן

Baruch Atah Adonai
בָּרוּךְ אַתָּה יְיָ

Magein Avraham [ufokeid/v'ezrat Sarah]
מָגֵן אַבְרָהָם [וּפֹקֵד/וְעֶזְרַת שָׂרָה]

Please be seated.

May God, who brings peace to the universe, bring peace to us and to all of Israel.

Oseh shalom bimromav	עֹשֶׂה שָׁלוֹם בִּמְרוֹמָיו
Hu ya'aseh shalom aleinu	הוּא יַעֲשֶׂה שָׁלוֹם עָלֵינוּ
V'al kol Yisrael	וְעַל כָּל יִשְׂרָאֵל
[v'al kol yoshvei teiveil]	[וְעַל כָּל יוֹשְׁבֵי תֵבֵל]
V'imru amen	וְאִמְרוּ אָמֵן

TORAH SERVICE

Please rise and face the Ark.

Vay'hi Binso'a Ha'aron — וַיְהִי בִּנְסֹעַ הָאָרֹן

When the Ark traveled with the Israelites through the desert, Moses would say that, with God's strength, God's enemies would be scattered. The Torah will go forth from Zion and God's word from Jerusalem. We praise God for giving us the Torah.

Vay'hi binso'a ha'aron vayomer Moshe	וַיְהִי בִּנְסֹעַ הָאָרֹן וַיֹּאמֶר מֹשֶׁה
Kumah Adonai v'yafutzu oy'vecha	קוּמָה יְיָ וְיָפֻצוּ אֹיְבֶיךָ
V'yanusu m'sanecha mipanecha	וְיָנֻסוּ מְשַׂנְאֶיךָ מִפָּנֶיךָ
Ki miTziyon teitzei Torah x2	2x כִּי מִצִיּוֹן תֵּצֵא תוֹרָה
Ud'var Adonai mirushalayim	וּדְבַר יְיָ מִירוּשָׁלָיִם
Baruch shenatan Torah Torah x2	2x בָּרוּךְ שֶׁנָּתַן תוֹרָה תוֹרָה
L'amo Yisrael bik'dushato	לְעַמּוֹ יִשְׂרָאֵל בִּקְדֻשָׁתוֹ

Torah Tzivah Lanu Moshe — תּוֹרָה צִוָּה לָנוּ מֹשֶׁה

We rejoice that Moses received the Torah, which God commands us to follow.

Torah Torah Torah	תּוֹרָה תּוֹרָה תּוֹרָה
Torah Torah Torah	תּוֹרָה תּוֹרָה תּוֹרָה
Torah tzivah lanu Moshe	תּוֹרָה צִוָּה לָנוּ מֹשֶׁה

(repeat above 3 lines)

Torah Torah Torah Torah	תּוֹרָה תּוֹרָה תּוֹרָה תּוֹרָה
Torah tzivah lanu Moshe	תּוֹרָה צִוָּה לָנוּ מֹשֶׁה

(repeat above 2 lines)

Please be seated.

Eitz Chayim Hi   עֵץ חַיִּים הִיא

In this prayer, we compare the Torah to a tree of life for those who embrace it.
We ask for help returning to God.

Eitz chayim hi
Lamachazikim bah
V'tom'cheha m'ushar
D'racheha darchei no'am
V'chol n'tivoteha shalom
Hashiveinu Adonai eilecha v'nashuvah
Chadeish yameinu k'kedem

עֵץ חַיִּים הִיא
לַמַּחֲזִיקִים בָּהּ
וְתֹמְכֶיהָ מְאֻשָּׁר
דְּרָכֶיהָ דַרְכֵי נֹעַם
וְכָל נְתִיבֹתֶיהָ שָׁלוֹם
הֲשִׁיבֵנוּ יְיָ אֵלֶיךָ וְנָשׁוּבָה
חַדֵּשׁ יָמֵינוּ כְּקֶדֶם

CONCLUDING PRAYERS & SONGS

The order of the concluding prayers varies among different congregations.

Ein Keiloheinu   אֵין כֵּאלֹהֵינוּ

We thank and praise God and say that there is none like our God.

Ein Keiloheinu, ein Kadoneinu	אֵין כֵּאלֹהֵינוּ, אֵין כַּאדוֹנֵינוּ
Ein K'malkeinu, ein K'moshi'einu	אֵין כְּמַלְכֵּנוּ, אֵין כְּמוֹשִׁיעֵנוּ
Mi Cheiloheinu, mi Chadoneinu	מִי כֵאלֹהֵינוּ, מִי כַאדוֹנֵינוּ
Mi Ch'malkeinu, mi Ch'moshi'einu	מִי כְמַלְכֵּנוּ, מִי כְמוֹשִׁיעֵנוּ
Nodeh Leiloheinu, nodeh Ladoneinu	נוֹדֶה לֵאלֹהֵינוּ, נוֹדֶה לַאדוֹנֵינוּ
Nodeh L'malkeinu, nodeh L'moshi'einu	נוֹדֶה לְמַלְכֵּנוּ, נוֹדֶה לְמוֹשִׁיעֵנוּ
Baruch Eloheinu, baruch Adoneinu	בָּרוּךְ אֱלֹהֵינוּ, בָּרוּךְ אֲדוֹנֵינוּ
Baruch Malkeinu, baruch Moshi'einu	בָּרוּךְ מַלְכֵּנוּ, בָּרוּךְ מוֹשִׁיעֵנוּ
Atah hu Eloheinu, Atah hu Adoneinu	אַתָּה הוּא אֱלֹהֵינוּ, אַתָּה הוּא אֲדוֹנֵינוּ
Atah hu Malkeinu, Atah hu Moshi'einu	אַתָּה הוּא מַלְכֵּנוּ, אַתָּה הוּא מוֹשִׁיעֵנוּ
Atah hu she'hiktiru avoteinu	אַתָּה הוּא שֶׁהִקְטִירוּ אֲבוֹתֵינוּ
L'fanecha et k'toret hasamim	לְפָנֶיךָ אֶת קְטֹרֶת הַסַּמִּים

Please rise and face the Ark.

Aleinu עָלֵינוּ

In Aleinu, we praise God for making us
different than others in the world.
We bend our knees and bow to thank God, the Holy One.

Aleinu l'shabei'ach la'adon hakol	עָלֵינוּ לְשַׁבֵּחַ לַאֲדוֹן הַכֹּל
Lateit g'dulah l'yotzeir b'reisheet	לָתֵת גְּדֻלָּה לְיוֹצֵר בְּרֵאשִׁית
Shelo asanu k'goyei ha'aratzot	שֶׁלֹּא עָשָׂנוּ כְּגוֹיֵי הָאֲרָצוֹת
V'lo samanu k'mishp'chot ha'adamah	וְלֹא שָׂמָנוּ כְּמִשְׁפְּחוֹת הָאֲדָמָה
Shelo sam chelkeinu kahem	שֶׁלֹּא שָׂם חֶלְקֵנוּ כָּהֶם
V'goraleinu k'chol hamonam	וְגוֹרָלֵנוּ כְּכָל הֲמוֹנָם

Va'anachnu kor'im u'mishtachavim u'modim	וַאֲנַחְנוּ כּוֹרְעִים וּמִשְׁתַּחֲוִים וּמוֹדִים
Lifnei Melech malchei ham'lachim	לִפְנֵי מֶלֶךְ מַלְכֵי הַמְּלָכִים
Hakadosh baruch hu	הַקָּדוֹשׁ בָּרוּךְ הוּא

Please be seated.

Adon Olam recognizes the timelessness of God and God's relationship with us.
We put our spirits in God's hands and then have nothing to fear.

אֲדוֹן עוֹלָם אֲשֶׁר מָלַךְ בְּטֶרֶם כָּל יְצִיר נִבְרָא

לְעֵת נַעֲשָׂה בְחֶפְצוֹ כֹּל אֲזַי מֶלֶךְ שְׁמוֹ נִקְרָא

Adon olam asher malach b'terem kol y'tzir nivra

L'eit na'asah v'cheftzo kol azai Melech sh'mo nikra

וְאַחֲרֵי כִּכְלוֹת הַכֹּל לְבַדּוֹ יִמְלוֹךְ נוֹרָא

וְהוּא הָיָה וְהוּא הֹוֶה וְהוּא יִהְיֶה בְּתִפְאָרָה

V'acharei kichlot hakol l'vado yimloch nora

V'hu hayah v'hu hoveh v'hu yih'yeh b'tifarah

וְהוּא אֶחָד וְאֵין שֵׁנִי לְהַמְשִׁיל לוֹ לְהַחְבִּירָה

בְּלִי רֵאשִׁית בְּלִי תַכְלִית וְלוֹ הָעֹז וְהַמִּשְׂרָה

V'hu echad v'ein sheini l'hamshil lo l'hachbirah

B'li reisheet b'li tachlit v'lo ha'oz v'hamisrah

וְהוּא אֵלִי וְחַי גֹּאֲלִי וְצוּר חֶבְלִי בְּעֵת צָרָה

וְהוּא נִסִּי וּמָנוֹס לִי מְנָת כּוֹסִי בְּיוֹם אֶקְרָא

V'hu Eili v'chai go'ali v'tzur chevli b'eit tzarah

V'hu nisi umanos li m'nat kosi b'yom ekra

בְּיָדוֹ אַפְקִיד רוּחִי בְּעֵת אִישָׁן וְאָעִירָה

וְעִם רוּחִי גְּוִיָּתִי יְיָ לִי וְלֹא אִירָא

B'yado afkid ruchi b'eit ishan va'irah

V'im ruchi g'viy'ati Adonai li v'lo ira

19

3 Stars in the Sky

1 star in the sky, 1 star in the sky, 1 star in the nighttime darkness, 1 star in the sky
Is it time for Havdalah? No!— not 'til 3 stars shine above
So close your eyes and feel Shabbat, with us for its last few minutes.

2 stars in the sky, 2 stars in the sky, 2 stars in the nighttime darkness, 2 stars in the sky
Is it time for Havdalah? No!— not 'til 3 stars shine above
So close your eyes and feel Shabbat, with us for its last few minutes.

3 stars in the sky, 3 stars in the sky, 3 stars in the nighttime darkness, 3 stars in the sky
Is it time for Havdalah? Yes!— now that 3 stars shine above
So close your eyes and feel Shabbat, with us for its last few minutes.

1 star in the sky, 2 stars in the sky, 3 stars in the sky—*hamavdil bein kodesh l'chol.*

Hamavdil הַמַּבְדִּיל

In this song, we praise God for differentiating between things
that are holy and things that are secular.

Hama-hama-hamavdil x3

Hamavdil bein kodesh l'chol

Hamavdil bein kodesh, bein kodesh l'chol x2

הַמַ-הַמַ-הַמַּבְדִּיל 3x

הַמַּבְדִּיל בֵּין קֹדֶשׁ לְחוֹל

הַמַּבְדִּיל בֵּין קֹדֶשׁ בֵּין קֹדֶשׁ לְחוֹל 2x

KIDDUSH BLESSINGS

Before drinking grape juice:

Baruch Atah Adonai

Eloheinu Melech ha'olam

Borei p'ri hagafen

Amen

בָּרוּךְ אַתָּה יְיָ

אֱלֹהֵינוּ מֶלֶךְ הָעוֹלָם

בּוֹרֵא פְּרִי הַגָּפֶן

אָמֵן

Before eating challah:

Baruch Atah Adonai

Eloheinu Melech ha'olam

Hamotzi lechem min ha'aretz

Amen

בָּרוּךְ אַתָּה יְיָ

אֱלֹהֵינוּ מֶלֶךְ הָעוֹלָם

הַמּוֹצִיא לֶחֶם מִן הָאָרֶץ

אָמֵן

Before eating cookies or sweets:

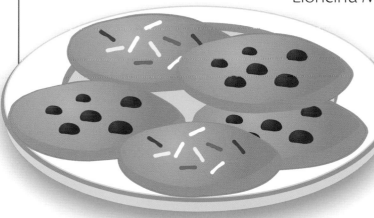

Baruch Atah Adonai	בָּרוּךְ אַתָּה יְיָ
Eloheinu Melech ha'olam	אֱלֹהֵינוּ מֶלֶךְ הָעוֹלָם
Borei minei m'zonot	בּוֹרֵא מִינֵי מְזוֹנוֹת
Amen	אָמֵן